Along the Bude Canal

Joan Rendell

Bossiney Books

First published in 1979
by Bossiney Books
St Teath, Bodmin, Cornwall
Designed, typeset and printed in Great Britain by
Penwell Ltd, Parkwood, Callington,
Cornwall

© *Joan Rendell 1979*

ISBN 0 906456 14 2

Plate Acknowledgements

Cover photography by Tony Bawden
Map   Paul Honeywill
6 - 9 courtesy of Bude Museum
43 courtesy of Mrs Mabel Petherick
All other photographs by the Author

ABOUT THE AUTHOR

The Bude Canal is — or was — a vanishing piece of Cornish history. As one more stretch goes under the plough or is built over, so another vital chunk of the Canal and Cornwall disappears. However now, thanks to the brilliant researching of Joan Rendell and her ability to get Cornish folk — related to the Canal — to talk, she resurrects it all. Moreover in doing so, she proves conclusively that history need be neither dull nor dusty. With considerable affection, she writes 'the canal will never die . . . it will never be forgotten . . .' and in this, her debut as a Bossiney author, she ensures precisely that. Through her words and pictures, we can see it flowing and working once again.

Born in Launceston, the daughter of a St Austell father and a Helston mother, she has travelled extensively: to every country in Europe — except Iceland — to the Middle East, North Africa and the Americas. Joan Rendell is a frequent lecturer and as a freelance journalist contributes to *This England, Devon Life, The Western Morning News*, and *Cornish Life*. She is the author of ten books on subjects as diverse as Matchbox Labels and Country Crafts, Flower Arrangements and Corn Dollies. Her passion for matchbox labels began at the age of eight, and her collection, now totalling 200,000 is one of the largest in the world. She lives at Tremarsh in the Parish of Werrington, through which the Bude Canal once flowed.

To my two Canal walking companions — John, who
helped me over hedges and ditches and ensured that
I didn't break my neck when unrecorded relics were suddenly
spotted in inaccessible places; and Zeus, who just went for
the fun of it and enjoyed every minute.

Also by Joan Rendell
Collecting Matchbox Labels
Matchbox Labels
Flower Arrangement with a Marine Theme
Collecting Natural Objects
Collecting Out of Doors
Country Crafts
Your Book of Corn Dollies
Your Book of Pressed and Dried Flowers

Along the Bude Canal

IN THE BEGINNING

It is probably true to say that the idea for the Bude Canal was born one day in 1814 in the lovely old Elizabethan manor house of Tackbeare, in the parish of Launcells.

There met, on that fateful day in 1814, two gentlemen, both landowners and yeomen farmers. They were very concerned about unemployment — a problem then just as it is today. Mr Braddon of Tackbeare invited Mr Harward of Newacott to his home to discuss ways and means of employing the poor. With the ending of the Napoleonic Wars, these unfortunate people had increased most alarmingly in numbers and in remote areas, such as the parishes of Launcells and Whitstone, there seemed little or no hope of ever alleviating, let alone eliminating, this distressing situation.

Mr Braddon had in his possession a report, made in 1793 by two engineers called Nuttall, on the feasibility of a canal running from Bude through poor agricultural land, probably to Hatherleigh. When suggestions for a canal had first been mooted, Lord Stanhope, a wealthy and influential landowner, had been enthusiastic and Messrs Brandon and Harward decided that Mr Harward should take the Nuttall report to London, consult Lord Stanhope and see if he would still be prepared to support the scheme.

The two men were delighted when Lord Stanhope pronounced himself agreeable and a meeting of interested, and presumably influential, people was planned for the following winter, to go thoroughly into the ideas for the project. But, unfortunately, Napoleon escaped from Elba, the war restarted and the meeting was never held.

Then in 1816 Lord Stanhope died and the plan could have died a natural death. However, Messrs Braddon and Harward were not deflected. They brought in another gentleman, Mr George Call of Vacy, North Tamerton, and then Mr Harward approached the new

5

Lord Stanhope who, according to C.S. Gilbert in his *Historical Survey of the County of Cornwall* published in 1820, immediately 'honoured the plan with approbation'.

As a result, engineer James Green and surveyor Thomas Shearm were asked to survey a line for the canal.

After various ups and downs, an important meeting of subscribers to the project was held at Launceston on 5 November 1818 and finally, after many abortive suggestions, an Act of Parliament was obtained in 1819 and The Bude Harbour and Canal Company was formed. There were three hundred and thirty shareholders, the principal ones being Lord Stanhope and his wife, Sir Thomas Dyke Acland, Sir William and Lady Call, Mr George Call, who later became the company's first chairman, William Arundel Harris and Sir Arscott Molesworth. Members of other prominent local families such as the Kingdons and the Cohans also subscribed, as did a number of Exeter businessmen gambling on what they hoped would prove to be a good investment. The Birmingham man, James Green, who had been connected with a number of projects in Exeter, was selected as engineer. Exeter was also the venue for the early meetings of the company, as its headquarters were in that city.

Once the Act was obtained on 14 June 1819 for construction of the canal, things moved quickly. Work officially began on 23 July 1819 and *The Exeter Flying Post* dated 5 August devoted a lot of space to a full report of the event. It certainly caused a stir in the quiet area through which the canal was to run!

Lord Stanhope travelled the considerable distance from his home in Kent and on arrival in Stratton his carriage was pulled into the centre of the village by local people, to the strains of a band playing stirring music and the cheers of crowds which had gathered. Lord Rolle provided venison for a banquet at Stratton in the evening.

At six a.m. the following day the church bells started ringing to herald the dawn of the canal age in North Cornwall and by mid morning twelve thousand people were estimated to be waiting on Summerleaze Downs at Bude for the festivities to start.

Bands led a procession headed by Lord Stanhope and Lord Mahon, a cannon was fired to signal its approach, and at the spot already prepared by James Green the first turf was cut by Lord Stanhope. The reporter from *The Flying Post* got quite carried away with the immensity of the occasion and the paper tells us that on Summerleaze Downs 'to commemorate these great events, there were

6

erected booths and also an immense and magnificent temporary structure covered with canvas and ornamented with evergreens and festoons of flowers'. The paper goes on to tell the excited public that the banquets, at which the viands were 'the best of their kinds', were held in the booths and that dancing continued for several hours. Elsewhere on the Downs 'various gymnastic exercises and feats of activity were performed, such as wrestling, running etc. etc.' Ten hogsheads of cider and 'many thousand cakes were given to the populace' and it must have been the biggest day Bude has ever seen.

When things really got under way, there was not enough local labour available to undertake the construction work and hundreds of navvies were brought in. Some, like the motorway construction gangs of today, followed the canals: when one was finished they moved on to another. Others were totally unskilled, veterans of the recent wars who were glad of any work and prepared to go anywhere. The men were paid between 1d and 3d a yard, according to the terrain and whether or not they were employed to fill carts. The cart-filling proviso was open to abuse and all sorts of conniving went on in efforts to claim the higher rate of pay.

The 'foreign' labourers were not generally welcomed by the local inhabitants. 'My door is barred to these foreigners, they are little more than savages' wrote a miller whose premises at Whitstone were so close to the canal that he feared for the safety of his mill stream and the continuance of his business.

From the few surviving contemporary writings by ordinary folk it would appear that people over whose land the canal was to be cut were not very fully consulted. Consequently there was a great deal of bad feeling and dissatisfaction. Complaints poured into the Canal Company's office. Farmer Brummell went out one morning to inspect his field of oats at Vealand, on the Holsworthy branch, and found it being bisected by a gang of men 'digging furiously'. For this damage he claimed £2.10.0. and in that area feelings became very sour with the Canal Company and its works.

The Holsworthy branch seems to have come off worst in the matter of damage; perhaps by the time they started on the Launceston branch the Company and its workers had learnt from experience to be more careful. Farmer Piper of Burmsdon had a horse killed when it fell into a deep cutting and he claimed what now seems the ridiculous sum of £1. Farmer Richard Lyle of Cross threatened to summons the person who drove a cart through his field of clover and everybody seemed to be losing their animals and finding other people's trespassing on their land. In Colehill Wood, Boyton, at the extremity of the Launceston line, it was claimed that streams were diverted and good husbandry threatened by this action.

With such acrimony and hindrance, it is remarkable that any work ever got completed at all, but completed it was. The Launceston branch was opened only a year after construction commenced — rather astonishing in those days when every inch had to be dug by hand for bulldozers and earthmovers had never been dreamt of then.

The canal was constructed for the prime purpose of conveying sea sand from Bude for use as fertiliser on the farms inland, much of the land then being of poor quality. It was also intended to carry other merchandise as well and in the latter years of operation the canal carried larger quantities of goods other than sea sand.

It was originally intended that the canal end at Ridgegrove near Launceston but the Duke of Northumberland, then resident at Werrington Park, refused to allow it across his land and instead it terminated at Druxton, over three miles from Launceston.

HOW IT WORKED

There can be no doubt whatsoever that the Bude canal was an ingenious undertaking. It was unique — the longest ever built to be worked by tub-boats. No other had as many as six incline planes and no other reached the dizzy height of 350 feet from sea level within six miles.

It was, in effect, an amphibious railway; the tub-boats had iron wheels on them and at the incline planes they were floated right out of the water and placed on rails, becoming railway trucks until they reached the top or bottom of the plane. Then they would go into the water again! This method of working was a substitute for locks and the rails ran into the canal at both ends of the plane, so that the boats automatically floated off. Each plane had two sets of rails so that boats could ascend and descend at the same time.

It took approximately five minutes for a boat to be raised up the plane but the downward passage was much faster. The late Mr A.W.

SAND BARGE - TUB BOAT.
Used
on Bude Canal.
Raised in 1976 after 90 yrs. submersion
FURTHER INFORMATION IN BUDE EXHIBITION

1. Tub-boat dredged from the canal near Bude — now exhibited at Bude Museum.

2.   The sea lock at Bude.

3. The entrance to the sea lock at Bude showing the bridge built to carry the sand tramway.

4. The lines of the sand tramway at Bude.

5. What was Sir Thomas Acland's private wharf at Bude today.

Above: 6. Boating on the canal at beginning of this century. *below:*
7. The building of the swing bridge at Bude, 1887.

Above: 8. Tub-boats and barges lie idle or derelict at Bude — as the railway is built in the background. *below:* 9. In the days of sail at Bude - the upper basin and the bridge which replaced the swing one.

10 - 12. Three canal bound stones. *Above left:* a large one on the Holsworthy Line. *above right:* a smaller one with a piece chipped out possibly by trespassing cows. *below:* one built sideways into a wall outside Hele Bridge, Marhamchurch.

Rowland, who lived at Bridgetown, not far from the Werrington plane, recalled that the horses were always unhitched at the top of the plane and allowed to make their own way down to the lower level while the boats were being prepared to make the descent. The horses would wait at the bottom of the plane, but if they heard a boat coming down particularly fast — 'and the rattle was enough to wake the dead' — they would run away along the towpath for quite a distance, to avoid being drenched when the boat entered the water with an almighty splash!

The planes were worked by an endless chain over a winding drum, the boats being hooked on to the big chain and the motive power being provided by a water wheel at the top. All the planes worked by this method except the one at Hobbacott, the biggest and most complicated of them all. Known as The Great Plane, it was operated by two huge buckets contained in wells 225 feet deep. These buckets were suspended on a chain winding over a drum and alternately filled with water. A sixteen horsepower engine was also installed at the top of the Great Plane, for use in the event of the bucket mechanism breaking down — which happened frequently!

Such misfortunes were mainly due to the bucket chains breaking and sending the buckets crashing to the bottoms of the wells — a most frightening experience, as according to one contemporary report, 'you thought the end of the world was come'. Naturally, this greatly alarmed the horses and the grandson of one of the boatmen relates that 'they was racing all over the place tryin' to catch th' 'osses and th' men was scritching an' you'd 'a think they was down th' pit'. Hardly conducive to the smooth and efficient running of a business concern!

It was not only at Hobbacott that chains broke. The entire canal was plagued with breakdowns during the whole of its existence and breaking chains was one of the main frustrations. In the first six months of the working of the full length of the canal, repairs and faults cost the Canal Company over £2,000, more than the amount collected from traders for tolls for the entire year. Rails were frequently breaking and all wooden constructions seemed to be permanently rotten. In short, the materials, thought adequate, were unable to stand up to the strain required of them and this could have been due in some cases to economies practised by the Canal Company which proved to be uneconomic in the long run.

Much of the equipment was material which came readily to hand

and preferably 'for free'. All the bound stones were large smooth ones from the beach at Bude and on each was carved very beautifully 'BC 1839' at the cost of 1d a letter or figure. These large beach pebbles were also used as anchor stones but with a ring inserted in them. An exception is one found at Mr & Mrs Axford's Canal Farm at Tamerton Wharf, which is a dressed square of granite. Quite likely this stone was found lying about and was purloined for use as an anchor stone — another small economy. So the same could have been the case with much of the wood used in the canal construction. In all the wharf buildings — stores and stables — the timbers are roughly cut tree trunks: one gets the impression that they were hacked down because they were near at hand and used at once.

Leaks in the canal were a constant bugbear and slipping banks were another menace. The latter mishaps arose largely through the carelessness of the boatmen, some of whom were not only careless but plain inefficient at their job. These men were recruited because they happened to live near the line but they had never before in their lives even been in a boat, let alone did they know how to handle one. Naturally, there were exceptions to the rule and some of the boatmen were very skilful, but the majority were not.

The tub-boats were strung together four or six at a time, each 'string' being drawn by one horse. The leading boat had a pointed bow and the boatman stood in the bow of the second boat to steer the whole string. To do this he was equipped with a handspike which he wielded between the first and second boats to control their passage. Some boatmen used their own 'bar irons' or even 'pikes' (two pronged hay forks), usually because they had dropped the official handspike overboard at some time. When the canal was drained or dried up dozens of these handspikes were found on the canal bed at one point and another.

This rough and ready method of steering meant that the boats frequently banged from side to side against the banks and, as each boat had heavy iron wheels, these gouged out whole chunks of the bank.

This rather crude method of transportation did not include many safety features. The only one was an iron bar fitted in the stern of each boat, which was intended to be forced into the ground in the event of a chain breaking or any other such accident on the planes. It was supposed to stop the boats from running backwards — presumably there was nothing to stop them running forwards! In the event there was seldom time to apply this 'brake' when a chain snapped suddenly.

So careless were some of the boatmen and so acute the damage that Mr George Call, the Company's first chairman, personally cautioned the boatmen in 1827 and recommended that stone walls and coping should be built at some sharp bends in order that boats inaccurately steered would not plough into the banks. Near the sharp bend at the boundary of Braggshill Wood and Bradridge Woods in the parish of Boyton there are still lying on the towpath some enormous square blocks of worked stone which are believed to have been intended for this purpose at that spot. Whether or not they were ever used is not known.

According to Davies-Gilbert in his *Cornwall Parochial History*, published in 1838, damage by tub-boat wheels was so extensive that in 1837 they were enclosed on each side, so that they only projected very slightly below the lower surface.

Winter brought great trials to the canal. Ice was a terrible hazard. Once the canal was frozen nothing could travel and even less severe frosts brought disruption. At the Werrington plane huge water containers were kept boiling on open fires, the boiling water being thrown down to thaw the ice on the rails. In cold weather tub-boats carried a heavy, long-handled, clawed sledgehammer which was used as an ice breaker.

In summer there was another hazard. Drought sometimes caused the level of the reservoir to drop too low to service the canal and the canal had then to be closed. It was also closed at harvest time because farmers were too busy to collect goods from the wharves and canal employees were needed to work on the land. The winters also brought floods and then the canal could overflow. In May 1831 the flood waters rose so suddenly that sand was washed off the wharves at Blagdonmoor and Hele Bridge and in 1835 the aqueduct over the Tala Water at Bridgetown was washed away by floods; only two isolated incidents in a series caused by the elements throughout the working life of the canal.

Skating on the canal was a great pastime for local people and many can recall hours of pleasure spent in that way after the canal closed.

In the heyday of the canal all the wharves were very busy. 'The Manure Season' was extensively advertised in the local press in the 1860s by firms who had stores at the wharves. William Soby, the wharfinger at Druxton during part of that time had his hands full and on a memo obviously intended for his assistant he scrawled 'If Northey wants free delivery, to be acquainted with charges and turned away if refuses'. Today one would think that the Mr Northey in question was certainly penny-pinching if he refused to pay the delivery charges then in force! A. Shepherd advertised 'Coal at Druxton Wharf 20s per ton. Newcastle and other kinds of screened will be charged 1d per cwt. higher. Charges for delivery of coals in Launceston and St. Stephens from Druxton 3s per ton or 2d per cwt. for quantities less than a ton.' At the same time sand was being offered at Druxton at 'per seam 5½d cash, 6d credit'; manure salt was 18s per seam. There were frequent complaints from farmers that the price of sand conveyed by the canal was too high and presumably Mr Northey was one of these.

During that important 'Manure Season' Joseph Spettigue, manure merchant, of Whitstone Barton, Holsworthy, took an extra large space in the *Launceston Weekly News* and begged 'to inform his Friends and the Public generally that he has received a Supply of the best Peruvian Guano. Available at stores Hele Bridge, Tamerton Wharf, Blagdon Moor Wharf and Druxton Wharf.' If today the stores look to us to be very small it must be remembered that sand, coal and culm were often stored on the wharves in the open. Some merchants had stores at only one wharf. Short & Orchard of Launceston based all their coal and manure at Druxton and Hender, Peter & Co. of Launceston made quite a display there, having 'on show and sale a large quantity of Bude Sea Sand, Coal, Grindstones, etc. etc.'.

The first traders to use the canal were B. Adams, S. Bray, H. King and H. Rundle and the number gradually increased, although some 'fell by the wayside'. The Canal Company charged tolls for use of the canal and the traders generally regarded these as too high. As in modern times, the tolls increased every year and some traders contemplating taking their business off the canal were lent capital by the Canal Company in order that they might carry on.

It all appeared to be operated 'on a shoestring' and traders were often long overdue in paying their tolls. This, in turn, caused problems for the Canal Company and apart from a few boom years, the whole undertaking was more or less a struggle from the time of its inception until its closure and later abandonment.

In 1832 one of the original band of merchants, H. Rundle, sold his boats to Captain King and emigrated to America. Captain King was an officer in the Royal Navy and the canal's most distinguished customer at that time. He was, it would seem, the only one who paid his tolls on time and when in 1841 he was appointed Chief Commissioner to the New Zealand Company and gave up all his trading interests, the Canal Company was moved to send him an address, recording 'the honourable zeal' in the way he had 'so ably conducted the principal Mercantile Establishment of the Bude Canal'. Captain King also owned property which had become valuable by being near the canal and he sold to the Canal Company a cottage at Druxton Wharf for £150 and also his stables and coal stores at Blagdonmoor and Stanbury Wharves. These were later rented from the Canal Company by Ham & Co. All the traders had iron stakes with their initials to mark their own trading areas at the wharves.

Although the early traders were very lax in paying their tolls — presumably using the excuse that trade was so bad that they could not meet their commitments — others were always ready to take their places. As King and Rundle dropped out so in 1841 came John Somers, James & Co. and the Bude Canal Trading Company. In the 1850s and '60s Short & Orchard, A. Shepherd, Hender, Peter & Co. and Joseph Spettigue all had stores at Druxton and Spettigue also had stores at Hele Bridge, Tamerton and Blagdonmoor. Thomas Brown and Davey & Son were active at the Bude end of the canal.

In the 1870s Vivian & Son, 'dealers in coal, sea sand, culm and artificial manures', had practically the monopoly at Stanbury Wharf, Holsworthy. They also held the distinction of being the last traders on the canal, operating right up to 1888, although in the last year only on a temporary basis. They were even made the whipping boy and blamed largely for the collapse of the Canal Company because, it was claimed, they refused to drop the price of sand by 4d a ton although they would still have made a good profit.

By 1866 several of the merchants who had used the canal were already advertising their goods being brought to the area by rail. In order to try and boost the trade in sea sand in the autumn of 1865 Short & Orchard included in their advertisement in the local paper a 'Copy of a Letter from Dr. Voelcker, Professor of Chemistry, To the Royal Agricultural College, Cirencester' in which he gave 'a careful analysis of Shell Sand from Bude'. By the end of 1865 Short & Orchard were the only traders advertising their service via the canal in the local press. In 1877 Hender & Co. was the only firm recorded in the Parish Book for Werrington — kept by the then vicar, Rev'd G. B. Gibbons — as paying a subscription to Werrington School. They were listed as 'Hender & Co Canal Comy Rateable £22.10.0 Sub. at 2d in the £ 3/9'.

In the early days of the canal the number of employees was modest. Nineteen were employed in 1830 and these included a lock keeper at Bude, wharfingers, planekeepers, who also did odd jobs on maintenance work and even acted as boatmen at times, and mechanics and masons who were required to travel to whichever place on the canal required their services. But in the 1840s the canal provided direct employment for somewhere in the region of one hundred people. It appears that the Canal Company even had some form of incentive scheme for its workers — one old man says his grandfather referred to it as 'a competition' — because in 1841 it was resolved 'That the sum of ten shillings be paid to the labourer whose portion of canal shall at the expiration of one year appear to Mr. Vowler to be in the best order'.

Throughout its existence canal wages were nothing to write home about. In 1837 Charles Brown, described as the 'conduiter' at Hobbacott plane, received 3s 6d a day, with a cottage, and his assistant Thomas Shepheard had 3s a day, also with a cottage. William Dyer the mason was paid 2s 3d a day, as was George Bond the wharfinger at busy Hele Bridge. Thomas Brown Jnr, the carpenter, had only 1s a day but in 1878 wages had increased for some and dropped for others; James Sleeman, the then carpenter, received 19s a week — the craftsman's wage.

John Balsdon was blacksmith to the company from 1837 to 1887, fifty years of devoted service, yet his wage rose only from 17s to 19s during the whole of his long period of employment.

They were versatile fellows, the men who worked on the canal. For instance, James Collom joined the company in 1834 as a clerk at Bude and remained such until 1862, but he also carried out duties as a wharfinger at Hele Bridge during busy times in the 1850s. His original salary was £85 per annum but this was reduced to £45 per annum in 1859, despite the fact that he was carrying out extra duties as a wharfinger. Who would today suffer a massive cut in salary like that and yet continue doing extra work?

Another who could turn his hand to almost anything was James Sleeman. He worked on the canal from 1873 until the mid 1880s. He was employed as a carpenter at the 'craftsman's wage of 19s per week' but he was also the canal handyman for many years. In 1882 he also became planekeeper at Hobbacott, where he lived, taking over that job on the retirement of Charles Brown Senior, who had, during his period of employment, progressed from conduiter to planekeeper. James Sleeman was a man of sober and industrious habits: it is said that in his spare time his life centred on the Band of Hope movement. He was a typical example of the industrious canal worker who moved at his own pace but it was an unending task. As soon as one job was finished to put the canal in perfect working order something else would go wrong and it was back to square one again for James Sleeman and his fellow workmen.

Although they worked hard the skilled men among them could proceed at a leisurely pace: tools in those days did not achieve such speedy results as modern aids. To take an example, James Sleeman recorded in a personal diary the sawing of a brake for Tamerton plane; the work took three days and then there were another three days of sawing for a frame around the shaft. While this was going on traffic was either halted or curtailed, according to the nature of the repairs required.

But whilst the Canal Company was niggardly in payments to employees, it was generous to its customers, especially the good ones. It entertained the most important farmer customers to dinner when they paid their accounts and apparently no expense was spared. Richard Palmer farmed at Headon, near Holsworthy, and at Wilsworthy, Tamerton, and had many seams of lime and measures of sand for use on his land carried from Bude by canal. Still in existence are some bills received by him from the Canal Company for several years from 1873 onwards, couched in terms such as 'Pay Day, Wed. 28th November. Dinner at 2 o'clock'. On 15 January 1873 dinner was provided at the Stanhope Arms, Holsworthy for those paying accounts of over £3 but in subsequent years the meal was provided at the inn which once existed at Dolsdon, on the edge of Tamerton parish, and which is now a farmhouse.

However, by that time even the offer of a hearty free dinner could not woo enough customers. With the excitement engendered by the coming of the railway, many people not only lost interest in the canal, they seemed to want to do their utmost to discredit it, even to get rid of it. It suddenly got blamed for all sorts of things, especially by the influential and more well-to-do people. Perhaps one of the most strange was an allegation that it could be instrumental in spreading the cattle plague!

On Saturday, 10 February 1866 a public meeting was held at

Launceston concerning a case of cattle plague — foot and mouth disease, as it is known today — which had occurred on a smallholding in Werrington the previous week and which was causing considerable disquiet. A Mr R. Peter jumped to his feet during the excitable meeting and said that 'a dog belonging to a man on the canal was given to straying' and as there were 'suspicious cases near Bude' the disease might have been spread by that dog. Another person at the meeting questioned the likelihood of the dog wandering as far from its home as Bude, whereupon Mr Peter coped admirably by saying that the dog was in the habit of riding in the boats on the canal!

THE BUDE TO RED POST LINE

To visitors who flock to North Cornwall in the summer months the Bude Canal is represented by the two mile section of comparatively wide waterway, with well maintained towpath, seats at specially scenic points so that weary walkers may rest their legs, swans and ducks on the water and sometimes even rowing boats and fishermen.

But this stretch is not the complete picture of the Bude Canal, even in its heyday. Originally the two miles of the canal to Hele Bridge were intended to be wide enough and deep enough to facilitate the easy passage of barges carrying forty tons of sand. The estimate was a bit ambitious and in the event barges with a capacity of only twenty tons were used, but all the same they were quite impressive.

The building of a breakwater from the mainland to Chapel Rock at Bude was an important point to be considered and the major construction at the start of the canal was the sea lock, on which work commenced in 1819. On 5 March 1821 the water was let into the basin at high tide and during the following weeks the Company's inspector, John Kingdon, carried out several experiments in loading the first boat with sand. On 21 April 1821 Mr Kingdon recorded in his log book 'Took the Barge No. 1 out the Sea Lock and put on board her about 24 tons of sand pm at tide time got her into the Basin, the Barge drawing 3ft 6in aft and 2ft 10in forward'. These barges, measuring 50 feet by 13 feet by 3 feet 6 inches, could only travel the canal as far as the wharf at Hele Bridge. There the merchandise

13. Mr W.H. Gregory of Bude with three tub-boat wheels dredged from the canal, near Rodd's Bridge.

Above: 14. The three tub-boat wheels with axles and fragments of tub-boat still adhering to them. *below:* 15. An iron wheel still attached to the remains of a tub-boat in Exeter Maritime Museum.

Above: 16. Winding machinery from Whalesborough Lock and tub-boat building tools. *below:* 17. A big Bude beach pebble used as a mooring stone.

Above: 18. The barge canal looking towards Rodd's Bridge. *below:* 19. Rodd's Bridge lock on the Bude-Hele Bridge stretch of the canal.

Above: 20. The canal today between Hele Bridge and Marhamchurch incline plane. *below:* 21. Hele Bridge.

Above: 22. The house of George Casebourne, the canal engineer, at Hele Bridge. *below:* 23. Storehouses at the site of the basin at the top of Hobbacott incline plane.

Above: 24. Model in Bude Museum of Hobbacott incline plane in its working days. *below:* 25. A grassy slope — once the impressive Hobbacott incline plane.

26. The first mile post near Rodd's Bridge still in place.

was transferred to tub-boats for the rest of the journey on the narrower, shallower reaches of the canal. Some tub-boats went direct to the main basin at Bude to be loaded, especially when sand was to be the cargo. A miniature railway was laid, together with its own little iron bridge and turntable, to convey sand to the basin for loading, the small sand trucks being pulled by horses.

Sir Thomas Acland had his private wharf above what is now Falcon Bridge, which replaced the original swivel bridge, and the sturdy warehouses still stand today, forming a picturesque background to the waters of the canal.

There were two locks on the two mile stretch to Hele Bridge: Rodds Bridge and Whalesborough — today a forlorn sight, devoid of gates and mechanism and with the upper gates replaced by concrete spillways. The canal is also now overgrown and muddy beyond Rodds Bridge itself.

1838 was a disastrous year for the canal. A violent storm almost completely destroyed the breakwater, wharves were flooded and goods washed away, aqueduct parapets damaged and the aqueduct at Bridgetown washed away altogether.

But at Bude the canal knew both sad and happy occasions. If the Canal Company was at one time in despair at another it was 'on top of the world'. On 31 January 1865 the tide was higher at Bude than it had been for twenty years and according to the *Launceston Weekly News* 'great fears were entertained that the lock gates would be smashed by the heavy runs, but fortunately they held together'. The sand tramway was completely ripped up, however, and the sea wall protecting the locks and banks of the canal was all but destroyed, the damage sustained by the Canal Company being estimated at 'but little short of £200'.

What a different story the same paper had to tell on 29 April of the same year: 'On Thurs afternoon the schooner "Ellen Martin" was launched from the yard occupied by Mr. Stapleton into the Bude Canal. The afternoon was exceedingly fine and many spectators were present to witness the event. The launch itself was an exceedingly pretty sight and passed off quite successfully.'

On August Bank Holiday 1928 one of the big attractions of the day was aquatic sports on the canal, organised by Bude Football Club — there were happy times on the canal again.

Hele Bridge Wharf was a very important place in the working days of the canal. The situation was pleasant; the canal and river Strat ran side by side, the spot was sheltered and here the canal engineer's house was sited, a high, strong wall built partially of Bude beach pebbles protecting the grounds of the house from the canal towpath. On the other side of the road the engineer had a reserved mooring for his own personal barge, by which he travelled to inspect the canal, and woe betide anybody who was imprudent enough to tie up alongside! That basin has long been filled in by tipping but the area of rough grass which now covers it is still regarded as the responsibility of the occupier of the engineer's house and is mowed and kept tidy by that person, although the large house has now been converted into three flats.

George Casebourne, the canal engineer from 1832 to 1876, was the most notable resident of the house. He succeeded James Green and was apparently an influential and highly regarded personality. He served the Company for forty years and died 'in harness' in 1876, after which the Canal Company bought his widow's house at Hele Bridge and granted her the sum of £50, a generous gesture on their part.

One story about Mr Casebourne is that at hectic moments during the working of the busy wharf, with boats jockeying for position alongside and cargoes being transferred from barges to tub-boats, he could be relied upon to raise his head above his garden wall and shout complicated instructions — often unintelligible because of the hubbub! — to wharfinger George Bond, who must have been sent nearly out of his mind by the unexpected and unwelcome interruptions which he had to obey if he was to keep his job. The uninhibited language of the boatmen and other employees when tempers became frayed was said to cause some distress to Mr Casebourne, who would put his hands over his ears to shut it out whilst at the same time yelling his own technical advice.

Mr Casebourne was succeeded by Nicholas Sullivan of Exeter, who took over at a salary of £12.10.0 a month. He also served the Company well and on 22 February 1896 the local press reported that 'A purse of gold was presented to Mr. N.E. Sullivan on his resigning the post of superintendent to the Bude Harbour & Canal Company'. It must have been very galling to Mr Sullivan when in June 1888 the Bude canal route was surveyed with the idea of it forming a railway line from Bude joining one of the existing lines to Launceston as part of the North Cornwall Railway extension and he was reported to have been 'greatly distressed' by the action.

Along the towpath from Bude is the cast iron one mile post still in situ; there were posts every quarter mile, the quarter mile ones being half the width of the mile ones. At Hele Bridge one of the old canal bound stones has been built into a wall, but on its side. What on earth possessed anybody to treat a lovely old relic in such a disrespectful manner?

The bound stones marked out the twelve foot width of the Canal Company's land and there were constant complaints that farmers were ignoring the boundary marks and in some cases were even tilling land right down to the edge of the canal. In order to combat this intrusion, mud dredged from the canal was tipped on the twelve foot width to assert the Company's right to the land, but the inspector still reported that cattle were being driven over the land and in some cases trampling bound stones. There is in existence today at least one bound stone with a corner and half of the number '9' on it long chipped off — presumably the result of being trampled underfoot by trespassing bullocks!

Not far from Hele Bridge was Box's Iron Foundry which supplied rails for the incline planes and doubtless much other necessary equipment, standing as it did in a strategic position at the foot of the Marhamchurch plane. The façade above the double doors has been rebuilt and a length of rail from the plane has been used to strengthen the masonry.

At the top of the plane the residents of the village of Marhamchurch never needed to travel to Bude to bathe in the sea. The section of the canal which ran by the bottom of the orchard of Court Barton Farm was a popular bathing spot.

The canal then continued to Hobbacott plane — described in chapter 2 — and so on to Red Post, where it branched, the Launceston line going off at right angles towards Merrifield plane in the parish of Bridgerule, the main or trunk line continuing to Holsworthy and being joined part way along by the feeder arm which brought the water from the specially constructed reservoir at Tamar Lake.

The Launceston-Kilkhampton road has a strange hump in it just before its junction with the Holsworthy-Bude road: this was formerly Thorn bridge, beneath which the canal passed. Right beside the bridge is a small bungalow, modernised but which could easily be mistaken for a former canal building. It was, however, there before the canal came and was a shippon and store. It was then converted into a bungalow by relatives of Mr Frank Bray of Launceston and Mr

Bray was told many times by his aunt how she and her brothers, as children, used to get into tub-boats which had been abandoned at Red Post after the closure of the canal and would pull each other along. Many hours of fun were enjoyed in that simple pleasure.

Nearby was a brick and tile works — perpetuated in the name of Tileyard Farm — and here were made most of the bricks used in the canal construction. Nothing remains today of the brickyard but a track alongside still consists mainly of brick rubble.

The Bude to Hele Bridge section of the canal still holds some memories for older Bude residents. The late Mr Bickle of Bude could remember being taken by his father, as a small boy, to see the last barge entering Hele Bridge Wharf. He recalled sensing even then that it was a sad occasion, the sort of ending, which although he did not understand it, affected his father to a noticeable degree.

The older folk still cherish memories and relics of the canal which played a very important part, one way or another, in the lives of their parents and grandparents. Another of Bude's senior citizens, Mr W.H. Gregory, a retired blacksmith and engineer, greatly values some fragments of the machinery of the lock of Rodds Bridge and three iron tub-boat wheels, still adhering to the fragments of the original wooden boat, which he dredged from the canal many years ago.

THE HOLSWORTHY LINE

On 8 July 1823 the first boats officially entered the water of the canal at Bude with merchandise bound for Holsworthy.

The Exeter Flying Post again had a field day, reporting the event in enthusiastic and flowery terms. It tells us that on this historic occasion 'That respectable and liberal character Mr. Blackmore, of Exeter, had the gratification of seeing launched on the waters of the canal, two barges of thirty tons each, and many boats, his property, and received on them manure and merchandize for Holsworthy.' After a further 'puff' for Mr Blackmore the report goes on 'The Committee of Management, supported by the neighbouring gentry, on the arrival of the loaded boats at the point of debarkation, marched through the town of Holsworthy in procession, the band playing "See the Conquering Hero Comes" and hailed by the acclamation of the populace of the surrounding country'.

Thus could Holsworthy rightly claim to be, as signs at the approach to the town proclaim today, a port town.

Now much of the Holsworthy line has completely disappeared, with stretches ploughed, turned into rubbish dumps or just completely grown over, but there are still some evocative relics remaining along the line and there are people still living who have tales to tell about it.

Mr E. Moore has lived for many years at Burmsdon and has long since retired from farming the land which his father farmed before him and on which was built the fine Burmsdon aqueduct and several other constructions for the canal.

Even today Burmsdon aqueduct over the river Tamar is impressive. Work started on 11 May 1821 and five men took two years to build it, completing it in the spring of 1823. The stone came from a nearby quarry and thirteen men were employed digging out and dressing it; the bricks were made at the busy brickworks on the banks of the canal at Red Post, the junction of the Holsworthy and Launceston lines.

Mr Moore has an interesting theory which he inherited from his father. He considers that the aqueduct was built on dry land and the Tamar later diverted to flow under it. This would have made the laying of the foundations and the actual building much easier and Mr Moore substantiates his theory by pointing to a stretch of sunken land nearby which is constantly waterlogged and which could conceivably have been the original course of the river.

Mr Moore has fond memories of the canal in his young days. He recalls moonlight skating parties in the winter and boating in the summer. He can vividly describe the weed-cutting operations which used to fascinate him as a child: a small boat would come along the canal, with one man pulling the boat and another standing up in it and wielding a long-handled scythe, cutting the weed as the boat moved along. When traffic ceased the canal was still maintained for several years and weed became a major problem. The process of cutting it was so slow that by the time the two-man team had got to the end of one line the beginning was getting choked again.

At Burmsdon Bridge it is still possible to see the grooves for the sluice gates which held back water from flowing to the aqueduct.

Burmsdon aqueduct, lovely today in its sylvan setting and most impressive despite the sad deterioration, saw tragedy in its time. A local story tells of a boatman 'in his cups' falling over the low parapet of the aqueduct one stormy winter's night and being drowned in the Tamar, which was in full spate. The horse plodded on alone, presumably unaffected by the incident, and was found many hours later standing patiently at a spot known as 'Cape Horn', a sharp U-turn near one of the two wharves at Virworthy. Its string of loaded boats was jammed tight across the canal, having been unable to negotiate the sharp turn without the aid of the boatman to navigate them, and it was not until the man's body was found, washed downstream, some days later that anyone knew what had happened to him.

One very old local resident, who declined to have his name recorded here, declares that the boatman's screams as he toppled from the aqueduct can still be heard on nights when the river runs in spate and engulfs the meadows on each side of its banks. He even claims to have heard them!

The first of the two wharves at Holsworthy was Stanbury Wharf, now completely overgrown and unrecognisable but with the warehouse and wharfinger's cottage still standing.

There a bridge carried what is today a main road over the canal and the boatmen knew a little trick to make their work at this point slightly easier. As the strings of tub-boats approached the bridge the men made the horses canter and the boats would then be dexterously detached: as they were moving quite speedily they would pass beneath the bridge with their own momentum and the horses would be coupled up again on the other side. The horses soon learnt this practice too and it is said that they would start to canter at the strategic point without any encouragement from the boatmen.

Vivian and Sons were the most important firm at Stanbury Wharf. They had their depot there and when, in 1879, the railway extended to Holsworthy and, surprisingly, was instrumental in increasing the sale of sea sand, Vivians rose to the occasion. To meet the demand in Stanbury Wharf's mini boom, they installed a weighbridge and opened an office at the wharf. The weighbridge was advertised as being of the latest advanced type and children would gather to see it being used, only to be chased off by the wharfinger wielding a big stick! In 1871 John Andrew became the wharfinger at Stanbury Wharf and he did such a good job that in 1878 he was promoted to take charge of the reservoir at Tamar Lake, a job which offered more regular hours but not much increase in pay.

The mini boom at Stanbury Wharf was short lived and its slowing down marked the beginning of the end of the canal business at Holsworthy.

Only a comparatively short distance further on was Blagdonmoor Wharf, actually the terminal point of the Holsworthy branch. Today the wharf is entirely grassed over, the houses which formerly belonged to the Canal Company are now farm dwellings, and stables and store buildings now shelter farm machinery and produce. But although the wharf area looks as though it could well be deep ploughed, Mr Ken Hooper, who farms there, has discovered that there is only three inches of soil above solid masonry — the wharves where the goods were unloaded.

The cobbled stable floor, stalls and drainage channel are still in excellent condition; it needs only one glance to see that they are Bude beach pebbles. When Mr Hooper came to live at the Wharf twenty years ago large lumps of coal were still found lying in corners of the former coal store.

One elderly man remembers his grandfather telling of one of the wharfingers at Blagdonmoor who was known by all the farmers in the district for his strict marshalling of the traffic at his wharf. John Gliddon served there from 1856 to 1866; he died in 1905 and is buried at Pancrassweek. He was a hard working, meticulous man who liked everything to run with almost military precision. He was very conscientious, ensuring that horses and wagons were dealt with efficiently by being directed on arrival to the most advantageous spot for loading their goods with the minimum of fuss and confusion. Some were told to wait for others to leave before entering the wharf area, others were told not to linger after completing their business. When Mr Gliddon was about there was no stopping your wagon as you entered the wharf for a gossip with your neighbour who was just leaving! Little did those farmers think that in years to come there would be people like Mr Gliddon, called traffic wardens, regulating the traffic in just the same way in nearby Holsworthy! However, the fact that such traffic regulation was necessary shows how busy the canal must have been in its heyday.

From Blagdonmoor Wharf the remains of the canal tail away for some distance into a deep cutting — part of ambitious plans which were doomed to remain little more than a dream. The log book of the Canal Company inspector, which recorded progress on the building of the canal, contains several references to 'the Tunnel', mainly in the period 1820-1821. The tunnel was a grandiose plan which never came to fruition. It was intended that the line should run from Blagdonmoor Wharf on to Thornbury and that this should include a tunnel. Many men were employed on the project and a great deal of effort must have been expended on it but, presumably because money was short, the canal never went beyond Blagdonmoor.

A fairly short distance from Blagdonmoor Wharf is the site on Vagglefield Farm where excavations commenced from east to west, with the intention of meeting the work being done from west to east. Today all that remains is a deep, overgrown pit — presumably the tunnel entrance — and a short stretch of the deep cutting. There is a curious legend attached to the east end of the proposed tunnel. The men working there complained that their boots were wearing out too quickly and they blamed it on something in the soil rotting the soles. Mr Heard, who has farmed Vagglefield for many years, says he has never found anything wrong with the soil and the navvies' complaint was quite obviously a ploy thought up by some bright spark to try and get a little something extra from the Canal Company. In those days a new pair of boots 'on the firm' was as good a 'perk' as a company car today!

ACTIVITY AT TAMERTON

Today North Tamerton could be described as a quiet backwater, a pleasant village, peaceful and calm. But when the canal was operating it was a very different scene; Tamerton then was a hive of activity, an important place to which came men, horses and wagons from many miles around, because Tamerton had a wharf with complementary buildings, an aqueduct and an incline plane, so that the canal dominated the scene and provided work for quite a number of the parish's inhabitants.

The road to and from Holsworthy was a comparatively busy one and it was crossed by an aqueduct which caused a great deal of exasperation to traffic using the road. Like all building on the canal the aqueduct was strongly built, as can be seen from the abutments which remain, but it was low and therein lay the trouble. Wagons piled high with corn or hay had to be specially 'trimmed' to go under

27.   Burmsdon Aqueduct on the Holsworthy line.

Above: 28. Holsworthy has every right to call itself a port town as it had two wharves. *below:* 29. The coal store at Blagdonmoor Wharf as it is today.

30 & 31 The warehouse and wharfinger's cottage at Stanbury Wharf, Holsworthy, today.

32-34. Graves of three canalworkers: John Gliddon, wharfinger at Blagdonmoor Wharf — buried at Pancrasweek; Samuel Parnell, boatman at Tamerton — buried at North Tamerton; and Noah Smale, planekeeper at Werrington — buried at Werrington.

In Loving Memory
of
NOAH SMALE,
THE BELOVED HUSBAND OF
MARY ANN SMALE,
OF WERRINGTON,
WHO DIED JAN^RY 5TH 1899,
AGED 56 YEARS.

A DEVOTED HUSBAND, A KIND FATHER.

GOD MOVES IN A MYSTERIOUS WAY
HIS WONDERS TO PERFORM.

WE KNOW THAT ALL HIS PAINS ARE FLED,
HIS TOILS AND SORROWS CLOSED FOR EVER:
WHILE HE WHOSE BLOOD FOR MAN WAS SHED,
HAS PLACED UPON HIS SERVANT'S HEAD:
A CROWN THAT FADETH NEVER.

ALSO OF MARY ANN, HIS WIFE
WHO DIED NOV^T 5TH 1904, AGED 64 YEARS.

Above: 35. Granite morring stone on original cobble stones which led to the stable at Tamerton Wharf. *below:* 36. The former coal store at Tamerton — now a bungalow. Coal was unloaded from the tub-boats up the steps and through the door on the right.

37. Mrs Emma Adams holding a portrait of her father — a
boatman on the canal.

Above: 38. Tackbeare Manor, the home of Mr George Harward, as it was when plans for the canal were made. *below:* 39. The canal as it is today at Boyton Bridge.

the aqueduct but it was the advent of steam traction engines which brought problems never envisaged when the canal was being planned and built. The high chimneys — the older residents never call them 'funnels' — had to be removed before the engines could go under the aqueduct and from all accounts the travelling fair which regularly did the round of Holsworthy, Camelford, Launceston and Tavistock was the worst affected by the canal's way across the road.

Even when the chimneys were removed from the fairground engines the lumbering machines could still not negotiate the low aqueduct and the men in charge of them would dig pits to lower the level of the road in order to facilitate movement of their paraphernalia. This performance was known as 'getting the road right' and there are still old people alive who recall how the air resounded with oaths and how crowds would assemble to watch the manoeuvre. One can imagine the state of the unmetalled road after such treatment — in those days there were no council workmen to be hurried to the scene by lorry to effect repairs!

This plague to road users remained for many years after the canal closed but it was finally removed. There are still vivid memories in North Tamerton of the day the 'akkeduct', as the old people call it, was brought down. Says one old lady who was among the crowd of local people who watched the operation: 'They unkeyed it the night before and the next morning early they knocked it down. I can remember it falling, it was some sight and there were heaps of carts there to take away the stones.'

The aqueduct linked the wharf and sand store on the north side of the road with the coal store on the south side and certain precautions had to be taken before the boats crossed it. There are constant reminders in the official records of the Canal Company that both the Company and the merchants who used the canal never made much money out of it. One contributory factor could well have been the recklessness of some of the employees, coupled with a slap-dash method of working. For example, when the tub-boats were loaded at Bude their cargo was apparently not weighed with any accuracy; the boats, it would appear, were just loaded until they were full and then sent off.

This posed problems further along the line and not least at Tamerton, where the aqueduct over the road had not been constructed with the working hazards in mind. When the boats arrived full of culm or coal at the wharf it was necessary to ensure that they were not overloaded because if they rode too low in the water as they went over the aqueduct they would cause such a wash that the water could cascade over the narrow towpath and low parapets and on to the road below. So a measuring device was kept at the wharf and this was put into the tub-boats to measure the weight of the cargo. If it was overweight the boatmen would merely toss the coal or culm out until the correct weight was reached. Huge quantities of both were wasted in that manner and to this day pieces can be dug up near the site of the wharf. It is said that one man who built a bungalow near one of the wharfs collected enough large lumps of culm to build a wall around his garden.

This practice of wastage, together with normal spillage as the cargoes were unloaded or as boats rattled down the planes, must have accounted for literally tons of culm and coal over the years. By contrast, when customers came to the wharf to collect their orders it was all carefully weighed before being taken away and the old lady whose parents were responsible for this checking of loads at Tamerton Wharf still has in her possession the original 7 lb and 14 lb weights which were used for the purpose.

It seems strange, in the light of today's materialistic world, that the canal employees who were existing on such pitiably low wages from the Canal Company did not retrieve all the wasted coal and culm, but presumably they had no use for it. On the other hand they could have sold it to farmers and others who *could* make use of it and it says much for the honesty of the country folk of that time that they did not exploit this illicit source of possible income.

Samuel Parnell was a boatman on the canal and lived with his wife and family in the wharf cottage, one of a cluster of three dwellings alongside the aqueduct. His daughter, Mrs Emma Adams, although now very advanced in years, recalls quite clearly stories told by her parents of life beside the canal in its heyday and has many fascinating tales to tell.

Mr Parnell, like most of the other canal employees, was recruited when the canal came to his own parish, in his case North Tamerton. As a boatman he was required to do two turns a day. This may not sound unduly arduous but it involved taking a string of boats on one short journey — from Tamerton Wharf to Druxton Wharf in Werrington, and then from Druxton right through to Bude — the long journey. After unloading at Bude he had to bring his string of boats back to Tamerton, fully loaded. Although this was known as 'one day's working' it was actually much longer because it took two days to travel from Launceston right through to Bude, or vice versa. So the boatmen bedded down with their horses for the night, at whichever stopping point they had reached. In very busy times work would continue through the night and then 'one day's working' could be stretched even further. At the end of a 'one day's working' the boatman had a day at home but that did not mean he could relax and do nothing for a whole day. That day had to be spent working his 'beat' of the canal — filling cracks, clearing weed, doing the hundred and one jobs of maintenance which were never ending. To say it was a hard life was putting it mildly but even so many boatmen and planekeepers did odd jobs in the hours when they were not actually needed on canal work. The boatman's task was not only guiding the boats and looking after horses, either. He had to help with unloading the tub-boats at the wharves and loading the wagons which came to collect the goods from his boats.

One of the biggest trials of a boatman's or planekeeper's life was keeping his beat of the canal 'watertight'. This was accomplished by going out with a bucket of clay and plugging all the cracks along his particular stretch of the canal.

For all this Samuel Parnell was paid 14s a week and on that princely sum he had to keep his wife and twelve children. To augment his income he did some gardening for an old lady who lived in a house nearby and when he was engaged on this work his wife had to take his place at the wharf and help load the wagons when the farmers came to collect their orders. Mrs Adams says that her mother ruined her health in the end by the hard work she had to undertake — 'lumping about great bags of coal and manure like a man'.

On such a small wage rearing a family of twelve children was not easy but one perk which the canal provided was a plentiful supply of eels. Mrs Samuel Parnell became very adept at catching these and would make them into pies to feed the family. Incidentally, when the last lay-by before the wharf was drained about fifty years ago Mrs Parnell's granddaughter, then a child, was greatly excited and has impressed on her mind for ever the sight of masses of eels which were brought out as the water was drained away.

The man who dug the huge hole to let the last water out of the canal at that point must have had very sad feelings as he carried out the work — the canal near there had claimed his son not many years before. Little Fred Mayne was only eighteen months old when he fell in the canal while playing on its banks and was drowned.

As the water drained out of the canal at Tamerton there came to light a long submerged tub-boat and that relic, in all probability unknown to the people who were watching as it was revealed, brought the wheel full turn in the story of the canal, for the old tub-boat was taken to Vacy, the nearby farm where George Call, one of the three men who had planned the canal, had lived.

Today the former sand and coal stores at Tamerton Wharf have been made into attractive bungalows, one of them occupied by Samuel Parnell's granddaughter and her husband. The old canal has been turned into a delightful sunken garden with the sturdy wharf walls still in situ. The original Delabole slate roofs are still on these dwellings, as good today as when they were constructed well over a hundred years ago. Part of the former coal store is now a garage but the massive beams and the stout door which was opened to allow the passage of coal from boat to store still remain. Another store on the opposite side of the road is also now a garage and a tiny shed incorporated in that building now houses a lawn mower, but when the canal was operational it was the wharf's 'public convenience'!

The canal will never be forgotten at Tamerton Wharf because relics of it are still coming to light. Dark red bricks in perfect condition are often dug up. These, like the coal and culm, are remnants of consignments of goods which were piled up on the wharf, ready for shipment, collection or sale. Much of the coal and culm, too, represents parts of loads which were jettisoned because the boats were overloaded for the aqueduct. The bricks came from the brick works which was situated just below the coal store at Tamerton. All the bricks were made by hand and Mrs Adams can remember the thrill, as a child, of being allowed to turn the handle in the brick works.

Fragments of tiles, chimney pots and other such things made at the brick and tile works at Red Post, where the Launceston line of the canal breaks away from the Bude-Holsworthy trunk, are dug up from time to time at Tamerton Wharf. While writing this book I was invited to come and see a length of heavy chain, with a type of anchor attachment on it, apparently still fastened to a long-hidden section of the wharf wall. This had just been revealed when Mr Brooke, the present owner of Haven Cottage and grandson-in-law of Samuel Parnell, was digging in his garden.

A mile or so on from Tamerton Wharf was Tamerton incline plane and an entirely different operation from the activity at the wharf took place there, as we shall see in the next chapter.

TAMERTON TO DRUXTON, WERRINGTON

About a mile along the line from Tamerton Wharf the canal reached the Tamerton incline plane, situated on land which forms part of Tamerton Town Farm.

From the top of the plane there are extensive views of the surrounding countryside and even today there is not a dwelling of any sort within sight. In the years when the canal was operational this must indeed have been a remote and lonely spot, with the only access across fields or via the canal itself. One would think that a man would need to be dedicated to his job if he took up residence, with his family, in such an out-of-the-way spot, but in those days there was not the demand to be near the facilities which are today taken for granted and, anyway, there was a lot of traffic on the canal, often by night as well as day, so there was no time to feel lonely.

Here, as at Merrifield, a waterwheel was housed in a beautifully built stone arched pit, and the machinery which worked the boats up and down the incline was installed in a cuddy. The incline plane was 360 feet in length and lifted the boats 59 feet.

Now only the arched entrance to the pit is visible — it is so overgrown with brambles and saplings and barricaded with tree branches to prevent animals from falling into it. But beneath all that undergrowth the masonry is mostly intact; like all things on the canal, it was built to last.

Close by the top of the plane the Canal Company built a cottage to be occupied by the planekeeper, and the first to hold that post at Tamerton was Thomas Smale, who came there in 1839. He was born and had lived in Werrington but was no doubt lured to Tamerton by the attraction of a new home and a steady job.

A legend grew up around Thomas Smale's wife. The story has it that Thomas added to his meagre income of 1s 8d a day from the Canal Company by occasionally doing work for local farmers — he is described in the church register as 'a labourer'. At such times his

wife, who was considerably older than him and apparently not able
to undertake heavy work, was left in charge of the plane. She
possessed a large bell; 'like a town crier's bell it were' says one old
man although he had never seen it and the story had only been
passed down to him by his father. This bell was one of the most
useful pieces of equipment which Mrs Smale had in the cottage.
When a miniature tidal wave coming round the bend in the canal
from the direction of Tamerton Wharf heralded the approach of a
string of tub-boats, Mrs Smale would go outside her cottage and
ring her bell with great vigour, whereupon Thomas would leave
whatever he was doing on the farm and would appear as if by magic
to carry out his duties of superintending the passage of the tub-boats
over the plane. It is strange that a simple thing should have made
such an impression that it has been handed down in parish history.
Probably it was unusual for a humble family such as the Smales to
possess an object which was presumably in those days something of
a status symbol. It could well have been that the Canal Company
provided the bell if Mrs Smale pleaded her frailty and inability to
work on the plane. Unfortunately no one knows where the bell is
now or even if it still exists.

Members of the fairly extensive Smale family came to be intimate-
ly associated with this section of the canal throughout its whole
working period and Thomas was particularly outstanding with regard
to his canal duties. From all accounts he was a very conscientious
and hardworking man and this was rewarded after he had been at
Tamerton four years, for in 1843 he was promoted to Werrington
plane, which had a better house and was not situated in such a
remote place. An entry in the Canal records reads: 'Thomas Smale in
charge of Tamerton line, increased from 1/8d to 2s per day as a
reward for his attentive conduct.'

But, sadly, Thomas Smale did not live long to enjoy those benefits.
The back-breaking hard work and the grinding poverty took their toll
and after only six years at Werrington he died in the Union Work-
house at Launceston at the age of only 56. He was buried in Werrington churchyard on 29 April 1849 near his wife, she having pre-
deceased him by only six months, also dying in the Union Work-
house. It was an ignominious end for a man so highly regarded by
his employers and who had served them so well.

All that is now left of the planekeeper's house at Tamerton is some
relics of the garden — an apple tree, almost touching the ground now

but still producing fruit, and a lilac bush which has outlived all the people who passed it daily when the boats were coming and going and Mrs Smale was scurrying about with her bell. Strangely, today, as one stands on that silent and remote spot and looks around the bend in the grassed basin of the canal, the people who came that way long ago do not seem so very far away after all; if they still hover around the remains of their once busy canal it is almost surely at Tamerton plane.

In the spring of 1978 the formerly grassed over Tamerton plane was ploughed for the first time and then some mementoes which had been hidden for eighty seven years came to light, turned out by the plough, rusty and corroded but still as strong and sturdy as on the day they were made: a ten link length of chain with a hook attached, a nail which had helped hold the planks of a tub-boat together, a long, double-headed bolt from a tub-boat, fragments of rail and one of the long bolts which had held down the rails, plus pieces of culm, coal and terracotta sherds spilled from cargoes as boats lurched over the sill of the plane and down the rails.

This section of the canal was not without its colourful characters and one of these was a man named Parnell (no close relative to Samuel parnell of Tamerton Wharf) who lived in a cottage high on a hill above where Braggshill Wood meets Bradridge Woods in the parish of Boyton.

Described as 'a big, rough man' he was recruited to work on the canal as a boatman. He did not have far to travel to work as his home overlooked the canal. He was renowned in the neighbourhood for his feats of strength and one story tells how he once demonstrated that strength by unhitching his horse from a string of loaded tub-boats and pulling the boats himself for a distance of several hundred yards along the straight, wooded section of the canal. There were some murmurings among the crowd that gathered to witness this performance that members of Parnell's family had helped to get the boats under way, so that they were moving more or less of their own momentum when Parnell was pulling them. But when Parnell offered to fight anyone who disbelieved his strength, the dissident voices were soon silent!

At Boyton Bridge there was another basin and wharf and a bridge took the road over the canal. There was no wharfinger's house and only some brick abutments remain to show that there was ever a bridge, but those who live there still remember the canal; a bound stone and a piece of chain have been built into the wall of a modern bungalow and Mr Sidney Dinner has in his garden nearby a curious iron contrivance, something like a chimney pot, through which tub-boat chains once clanked. It is now used as an ornamental plant holder.

William Barriball farmed at Tamartown in the parish of Werrington for many years. It was not a very large farm and as a young man, when things were slack, William did occasional work as a boatman on the canal, a little extra cash always being useful to a young man just branching out on his own as a farmer. He usually worked as a team with the boatman Parnell (he of the prodigious strength) and they would start off from Druxton Wharf at two o'clock in the morning with empty boats to be taken to Bude to be loaded. Much of the route was through wooded country and young William always found it particularly eerie plodding along in the middle of the night through the long stretch of the dense Braggshill and Bradridge Woods, especially if there should happen to be a thunderstorm. In such circumstances he was always very glad that he had the redoubtable Parnell with him, as the latter was strong enough and brave enough to ward off any spirits of long dead canal folk who might be lurking in the woods or making merry as the lightning flashed and the thunder rolled. This part of the line was, strangely, also one which the horses disliked and in bad weather two men were essential — one to steer the boats and the other to calm the horse.

One gets the impression that in those days thunderstorms were much more frequent than they are now, as in his latter years Mr Barriball's memories were often tinged with what happened on such nights when he had to travel the towpath from Druxton to Bude. What is more probable is that in the days when superstition was a part of every country dweller's life the young man felt genuine fear and dread of the unknown when travelling that stretch of the canal which, even today and in broad daylight, has a slightly sinister and 'creepy' air about it.

It is on the Boyton-Werrington stretch of the canal that there stands the most evocative of all canal remains. Hunch bridge is only an accommodation bridge between fields. Today it is silent and lonely, with human feet seldom walking over or under it, but it is in a remarkable state of preservation. Here, more than anywhere else, one realises the narrow width of the canal as one stands on the equally narrow path beneath it, on the very stones over which count-

40. Mr Ernest Barriball, formerly of Plane Farm, Werrington, with a 'big-end' — the chain which drew the boats up and down the plane, and a piece of one of its rails.

41.　The aqueduct over Tala Water at Bridgetown, Werrington. It replaced the original one which was washed away in the 1838 floods.

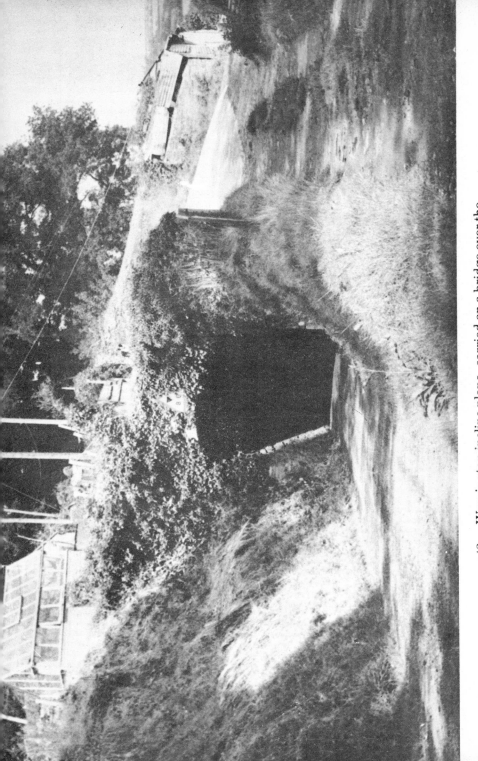

42. Werrington incline plane, carried on a bridge over the Bridgetown-Tamartown road.

43. Noah Smale's son Samuel with his wife and daughters, Elsie and Bessie, outside the planekeeper's house at Werrington incline plane. Samuel is holding the pony on which Noah used to ride his beat of the canal.

44. Hunch Bridge and towpath on the Druxton Wharf-Boyton Bridge section of the canal.

45 & 46. Druxton Wharf. *Above:* the basin now covered with rushes. *below:* the wharfinger's house.

Above: 47. The 20-mile post on the Launceston line — now almost hidden in undergrowth. *below:* 48. The canal now a sunken garden at the home of Mr & Mrs L. Brooke. The ivy covers the original wharf wall.

49.   Ridgegrove Mill, Launceston in the 1930s — where it was
intended the canal should end.

less horses tramped as they drew their loads along. Somehow that bridge, with its solidly built-up towpath, epitomises the canal and all it meant to so many people in those far off days. Standing beneath it one cannot fail to feel the atmosphere: the canal is no longer just a dried up ditch, instead pictures which seem disturbingly real are conjured up. Several people say that they have felt the same way at that particular spot.

The parish of Werrington has some of the best preserved relics of the canal. The incline plane built on a sturdy bridge spanning a parish road is still easily recognisable for what it is, although it now forms part of a farmyard.

The construction of the canal at this end of the line was not without problems, but it was after it actually started working that some rather unusual human problems cropped up. The Canal Company built for the planekeeper a house that is today largely unchanged from its original appearance, especially the exterior, and this was lived in by a series of planekeepers. The last of these was Noah Smale, who took over in the late 1880s, his forbears Thomas Smale and John Smale already having held the post in the even then distant past. But life in the house on the plane was not always easy. Its biggest burden was always snakes. When the canal was being built nests of snakes were disturbed: not just a few snakes but hundreds of them, and adders at that. Literally dozens of wheelbarrows full of snakes' eggs were taken away and destroyed but, despite the upheaval of their habitat, the snakes remained in the neighbourhood and until quite recently there were parts of the towpath along which people would not walk because the area was infested with snakes.

The snakes made life a misery for Noah Smale and his family. They were everywhere: they slithered into the house, getting in through the back of the open fireplace; they would be found in boots when the owners went to put on the footwear; on several occasions they even got into pans of milk scalding over the fire. But the greatest horror came one day when Mrs Smale was sitting by the fire, doing some sewing. She felt something tickling her foot and as she glanced down, expecting to see the cat touching her foot, she saw instead an adder sliding up her leg and underneath her long and voluminous skirts. The shock was so great that it made her ill, and her family were convinced that it actually killed her because she never fully recovered, dying not very long afterwards.

Mr & Mrs Noah Smale had a large family and the father carefully inscribed all their names, the dates and even times of their births in the family Bible. In those days maternity services were not what they are today and families had to make their own arrangements for the confinement in the best way they could. In the case of the Smales it meant calling upon a village midwife, one Mrs Cowling, who lived at Boyton Bridge, several miles away. Some of the Smale's children arrived in winter when the canal was frozen over and then Noah would fetch the midwife by taking the shortest route — along the frozen canal. He would propel himself along the ice using either a broom or a pike held in front of him and applied in such a manner that his progress somewhat resembled riding a scooter. His great niece recalls that after he had roused the midwife they would return the same way, she clinging with both arms around his waist or holding tight to his belt as he propelled them both along the frozen canal!

Noah Smale used to patrol his section of the canal on a pony, sitting sideways on its back and facing the canal, so that as the pony plodded gently along Noah could observe where the canal needed attention in the matter of weeds to be cleared, leaks to be plugged or banks to be repaired. As his family grew he also found the canal wages barely enough to keep them and the Canal Company allowed him to cultivate some small, rushy plots of land, at various points alongside his beat of the canal, to augment his slender income. As with so many of the canal employees he died at a comparatively early age; he was fifty six when he expired in 1899, eight years after the canal closed. Although most of the employees were given a week's notice to quit, Noah Smale was one of the lucky ones who was allowed to remain on in his home, the planekeeper's house at Werrington incline plane, and members of another branch of his family still lived there until recently.

Druxton Wharf remained busy almost up to the final closing of the canal and perhaps it was because the work was so arduous that there was a comparatively high turnover of wharfingers there. For instance, in 1859 it was George Northey, in 1861 John Crocker and in 1865 William Sobey. The last wharfinger was Mr Walter Smith and his son Walter, who as a young man helped his father at the wharf and died in April 1959 at the age of 81. He was the last surviving person who actually worked at Druxton Wharf when the canal was in being. He later turned to farming and for many years farmed Crossgate, which did and still does include Druxton Wharf itself, and it was there that he died.

Captain King, an officer in the Royal Navy, as mentioned earlier, sold a cottage at Druxton Wharf to the Canal Company for £150 and the latter used it to house the wharfinger's assistant.

Just over eighty years ago the bridge, which carried the rough road over the canal near Crossgates, was removed, the road was realigned and resurfaced and to one person, still living, fell the then unappreciated honour of making another little bit of local history. Mrs Mabel Moore, whose home is now in the neighbouring parish of St Giles-on-the-Heath, was the first person ever to travel on the new piece of road built over the former bed of the canal. But she did not set foot on it! She was only a baby and was pushed over in a pram, by her mother! Mrs Moore recalls that little story with a chuckle today. She says it was one of her late mother's favourite reminiscences, but little did that good lady ever think, when she was recalling it to little Mabel, that one day it would be recounted in a book! Mrs Moore remembers in later years Sunday School outings by boat on the canal from Druxton to Boyton Bridge.

There was also a second aqueduct in Werrington; it was at Tamartown but only the abutments remain today. It was taken down over sixty years ago, stone by stone, by Messrs John Sandercock and Bill Northey, two former workmen on the Coode estate, on whose land it stood, because it impeded the passageway of wagons loaded with hay and straw travelling the narrow road from Wilkey Down to Tamartown and beyond. In those days landowners were all powerful. They never had to think about conservation of ancient relics or planning permission and the estate employees had to turn their hand to anything — even removing canal aqueducts!

EPILOGUE

With every day that passes, the Bude Canal sinks further into oblivion. More stretches go under the plough or are incorporated in other land, built over or generally destroyed. Buildings deteriorate with time and become in danger of being demolished; questions arise over rights of way and portions of land are fenced off; all sorts of things can happen and the canal is no longer important to anybody.

Some of the kind people who provided information when the gathering of material for this book commenced have since passed on, taking with them the memories that meant so much to them and which it has been an honour to be able to record.

But the canal will never truly die; it was a great feat of engineering, a marvel in its day, and it served its purpose well. It will never be completely forgotten. Many of its remaining relics are earmarked for museums when the time comes for those who cherish them now to relinquish all worldly goods.

Dear Bude Canal! There are still those who remember and care — and there always will be.

ACKNOWLEDGEMENTS

This book has been a very personal one. It has relied for material not so much on official records and documents as on individuals, people with personal connections with the canal, all of whom have been so kind, helpful and interested in the preparation of this little volume. Everyone I have contacted has been very co-operative, people have gone to immense trouble to unearth family relics in the form of documents of all sorts so that I may examine them and extract matters of interest from them; others have shown and explained actual relics of the canal itself, or have searched their memories and recalled experiences from their childhood or stories told to them by members of their families in days gone by. All have been so friendly and willing that the writing of this book has been a tremendous pleasure and has resulted in my making many new friends.

To everyone I am greatly indebted for their help and especially to the following who have, among other things, allowed me access to their land, to examine features of their property and, in some cases, have walked with me to show special points of interest in the canal remains which were perhaps now unknown to anyone but them. These kind folk are Mrs Emma Adams, Mr & Mrs A. Axford, Mr Ian Ballantyne, Mr Ernest Barriball, Mr William Barriball, Mr Frank Bray, Mr & Mrs L. Brooke, Mr & Mrs H.J. Dauncey, Mr Sidney Dinner, Miss Iris Gliddon, Mr W.H. Gregory, Mr & Mrs C.L. Heard, Mr Ken Hooper, Mrs Kivell, Mr E.H. Moore, Mrs Mabel Moore, Mrs Oke, Mr & Mrs R.G. Parker, Mrs Mabel Petherick, Mr W.J. Rowland, Miss Maud Smith, Mrs Jean Sobey, Mr E.J.L. Spry and Mr M.A. Symons. Also I should like to thank the editor of the *Cornish & Devon Post* and the staff of the Western Studies Library, Exeter, for permission to examine files, the staffs of Launceston and Holsworthy Libraries for their help, the Reverend John Boatright and the late Reverend Robnett Walters for allowing me to examine church registers, and Mr David Clarke for his valuable help in enlarging photographs. Finally, I would like to thank Mr R. Hutchings, the former Curator of the Waterways Museum at Stoke Bruerne, Northants, for reading the manuscript and for his interest.

ALSO AVAILABLE

MY DARTMOOR
by Clive Gunnell of Westward TV — television's most famous walker. .
Map and 12 pages of photographs and drawings of Dartmoor wildlife by Robin Armstrong. Introduction by Jeremy Thorpe, M.P.
"The work is that of a merry man, and an observant, though kindly one."
Western Morning News

TOTNES
by Elizabeth Gunnell, 32 illustrations.
Elizabeth Gunnell follows the success of her Barbican story with an immensely readable guide about Totnes, one of the oldest boroughs in Britain.
"We meet historic people cheek-by-jowl with moderns . . . they all step out of the pages equally alive."
Devon Life

TIGHTLINES SOUTH WEST
A fishing guide to the south west by the popular Westcountry and Westward TV angler. Drawings and photographs — a mine of information for the angler, both local and visitors.
"A book with Tightlines South West as its title can only have been written by one person. And Ted Tuckerman doesn't disappoint us. He shares his vast knowledge of angling and where to fish our local shores and wrecks."
Jack White, Sunday Independent

THE BARBICAN
by Elizabeth Gunnell, 32 photographs.
"Anyone with a love for old Plymouth and the waterfront should not miss this lovely little book. It is outstanding value and highly recommended."
Tavistock Gazette

ABOUT EXMOOR AND NORTH DEVON
by Ronald Duncan, 15 photographs and map.
"You will find this book well-informed, well-written, well-illustrated and provocative." The John Blunt Column
". . . suggested routes across some of the loveliest stretches of the Westcountry."
Western Daily Press

TO TAVISTOCK GOOSIE FAIR
by Clive Gunnell. 41 photographs
A look at one of the historic Fairs in the Westcountry from the inside — the author himself lives at Tavistock.

CHARLES, DUKE OF CORNWALL
by Michael Williams, 30 photographs.
"This, the first ever publication about Prince Charles in his role as Duke of Cornwall is full of character and interest." David Clarke, Cornish Life

SUPERNATURAL IN CORNWALL

by Michael Williams, 24 photographs.

". . . a book of fact, not fiction . . . covers not only apparitions, and things that go bump in the night, but also witchcraft, clairvoyancy, spiritual healing, even wart charming . . ." Jenny Myerscough on BBC

"Serious students of ghost-hunting will find a fund of locations."
Graham Danton on Westward TV

MAKING POLDARK

by Robin Ellis, over 60 photographs.
The inside story of the popular BBC TV series.
". . . an interesting insight into the making of the TV series . . ."
Camborne Redruth Packet
"It is a 'proper job', as they say, and a credit to all concerned."
Archer in Cornwall Courier

POLDARK COUNTRY

by David Clarke, over 40 photographs.
Published in conjunction with Cornish Life Magazine: fascinating facts about the Cornish past, locations used for the TV series and interviews with Winston Graham and the cast.

MY CORNWALL

A personal vision of Cornwall by eleven writers living and working in the county: Daphne du Maurier, Ronald Duncan, James Turner, Angela du Maurier, Jack Clemo, Denys Val Baker, Colin Wilson, C.C. Vyvyan, Arthur Caddick, Michael Williams and Derek Tangye with reproductions of paintings by Margo Maeckelberghe and photographs by Bryan Russell.
"An ambitious collection of chapters." The Times, London

THE LIZARD

by Jill Newton.
". . . captures so well the magical atmosphere of the place, full of legend, restless green seas, crying curlews and sheltered byways . . . deserves a place on the shelf of any serious collector of Cornish books."
Pamela Leeds, The Western Evening Herald

CORNWALL & SCILLY PECULIAR

by David Mudd, 48 photographs.
David Mudd uses his perceptive eye and his pride of all things Cornish to write entertainingly, at times with humour, but always affectionately, of some of the people, events, values and beliefs that create the background to Cornwall's strange and compelling charm.

ALONG THE CAMEL

by Brenda Duxbury and Michael Williams.

". . . It is well written, attractively presented, full of historical facts . . ."
"Worth a place on anyone's bookshelf."   Western Evening Herald

ABOUT LOOE

by Austin Toms and Brenda Duxbury, 38 illustrations.

Austin Toms, a member of the well-known Looe family, talks about old Looe while Brenda Duxbury explores Looe and district today.

"A fascinating collection of memories."   Cornish Times
". . . a double-sided portrait of this double-sided town . . . draws together history, present and future of East and West Looe in one long-overdue volume."

Cornish Life

ABOUT MEVAGISSEY

by Brenda Duxbury, over 40 illustrations and map.

". . . an honest, detailed little study which doesn't just tell of a place but brings it gently and evocatively to life."   Western Morning News
"For lovers of Cornwall, About Mevagissey is a must."   Sunday Independent

HELSTON FLORA DAY

by Jill Newton, 48 photographs.

"The text of this delightful little book is well supported with photographs old and new."   Notes in the West

ALONG THE LEMON

by Judy Chard, 35 photographs.

". . . in prose and pictures, the story of the river from its rising near Haytor, its junction with the Sig and final pouring into the Teign."   Herald Express
". . . a book with exceptional sparkle."   Devon Life

HMS ARK ROYAL

by James Dalrymple, over 50 photographs.

". . . a superbly illustrated memento of the giant aircraft carrier up to her final return to Devonport. All the facts, the history, and many entertaining stories about Ark Royal are presented in a fast moving style."   South Devon Times